Learn to Read Sight Wo

This book belongs to:

_____

Reading & Writing can be fun! Loads of cheerful and interesting pictures for kids to color. Cutting & Pasting , Games & Activities will encourage kids to use this workbook.

This 100 essential sight words book helps kids learn to write and read high frequency words in a fun and engaging way.

It is organized in a progressively skill building way for kids to develop confidence to read and write.

Part 1:
    Learn to read and write 1, 2 and 3 letter words

Part 2:
    Learn to read and write 4, 5 and 6 letter words

This book may require guidance from a teacher, parent or care giver to help the child practice reading & writing.

Meet Jojo.
Jojo is a curious elephant.
He loves to learn and play.
Learn to read & write along with Jojo!

Hi!

My name is Sujatha Lalgudi. I sincerely hope you find my 100 Sight Words book to be helpful and fun.

Write to me at **sujatha.lalgudi@gmail.com** with the subject: **100 Sight Words** along with **your kid's name** to receive:

- Additional practice worksheets.
- A name tracing worksheet so your kid can practice writing their own name.
- An Award Certificate in Color to gift your child!

If you liked this book, please leave me a review on Amazon! Your kind reviews and comments will encourage me to make more books like this.

Thank you
Sujatha Lalgudi

Part 1:
Learn to read & write
(1, 2 & 3 Letter Sight Words)

- Say the word out loud & trace it
- Color the correct sight words.
- Cut out the word at the bottom of the page & paste it
- Write the word to fill in the blanks.
- Use the word in a sentence

*Remember: A sentence begins with a capital letter and ends with a period.

Are you ready?
Let's go!

⭐ Celebrate your success! ⭐

Color a star at the end of the book to mark each word you have learnt.

a

Trace the word and say it aloud:

A A A A A

A A A A A

a a a a

a a a a

Write the word on your own:

Color the spaces with the word:

Cut out the word at the bottom of the page and paste it here to complete the sentence:

I have [ ] cat.

Complete the sentence with the word:

I have __ cat.

Write your own sentence using the word:

a

Trace the word and say it aloud:

I   I   I   I

I   I   I   I

I   I   I   I

I   I   I   I

Write the word on your own:

Color the spaces with the word:

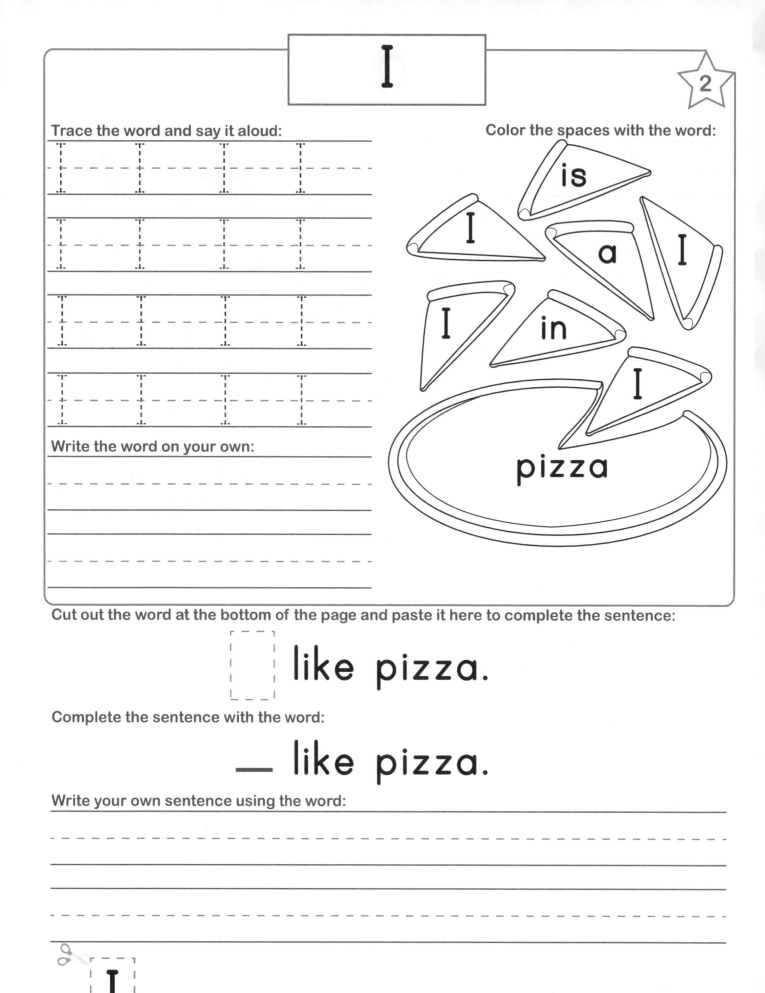

is

I

a   I

I   in   I

pizza

Cut out the word at the bottom of the page and paste it here to complete the sentence:

like pizza.

Complete the sentence with the word:

___ like pizza.

Write your own sentence using the word:

I

am

★ 3

Trace the word and say it aloud:

Am Am

Am Am

am am

am am

Write the word on your own:

Color the spaces with the word:

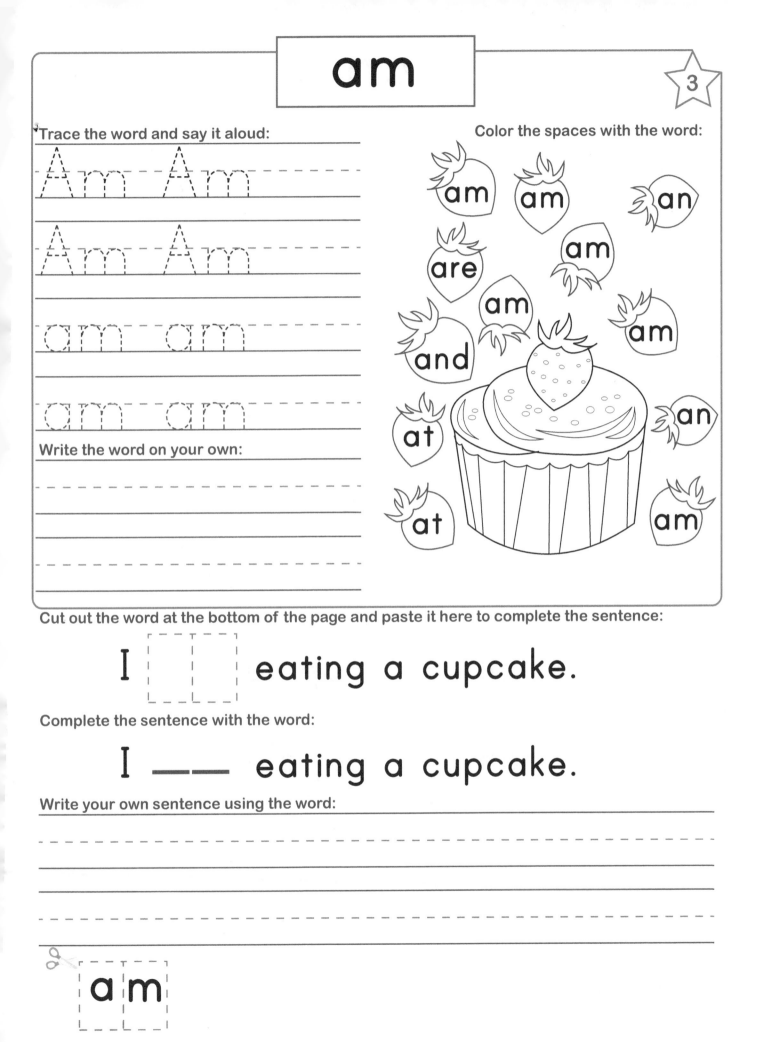

Cut out the word at the bottom of the page and paste it here to complete the sentence:

I ⌐ ¬ eating a cupcake.

Complete the sentence with the word:

I ___ eating a cupcake.

Write your own sentence using the word:

a m

an

Trace the word and say it aloud:

An An

An An

an an

an an

Write the word on your own:

Color the spaces with the word:

are

am

an

an

are

am

an

a

an

a

am

at

Cut out the word at the bottom of the page and paste it here to complete the sentence:

I see ☐ apple.

Complete the sentence with the word:

I see ___ apple.

Write your own sentence using the word:

a n

at

Trace the word and say it aloud:

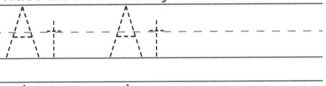

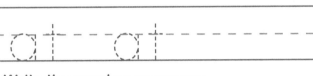

Write the word on your own:

Color the spaces with the word:

Cut out the word at the bottom of the page and paste it here to complete the sentence:

We saw a hippo ☐ the zoo.

Complete the sentence with the word:

We saw a hippo ___ the zoo.

Write your own sentence using the word:

at

be

Trace the word and say it aloud:

Be Be

Be Be

be be

be be

Write the word on your own:

Color the spaces with the word:

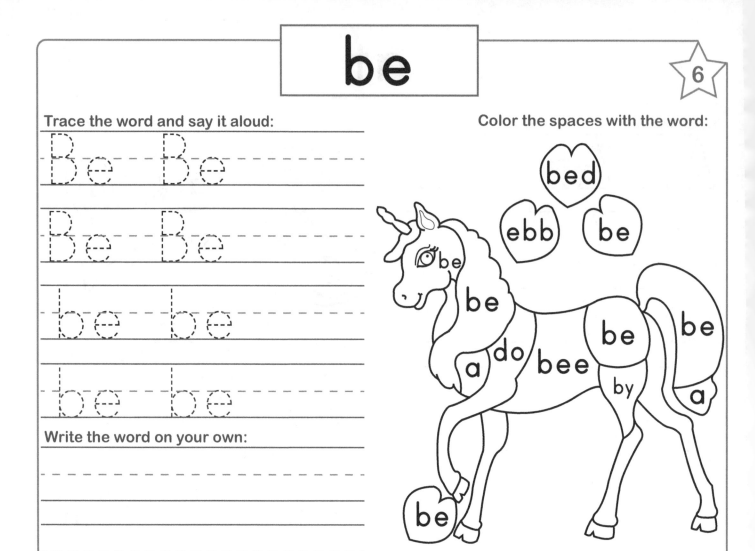

bed

ebb   be

be

be

be

be

a do   bee

by

a

be

Cut out the word at the bottom of the page and paste it here to complete the sentence:

Can you ☐ my friend?

Complete the sentence with the word:

Can you ___ my friend?

Write your own sentence using the word:

b e

Trace the word and say it aloud:

By By

By By

by by

by by

Write the word on your own:

Color the spaces with the word:

Cut out the word at the bottom of the page and paste it here to complete the sentence:

I go to school [ ] bus.

Complete the sentence with the word:

I go to school ___ bus.

Write your own sentence using the word:

by

go

Trace the word and say it aloud:

Go   Go

Go   Go

go   go

go   go

Write the word on your own:

Color the spaces with the word:

go   pogo   go

go

goo   go

ego

do   go

ago

gone

god   of

Cut out the word at the bottom of the page and paste it here to complete the sentence:

Can we [   ] to the park?

Complete the sentence with the word:

Can we ___ to the park?

Write your own sentence using the word:

g o

Trace the word and say it aloud:

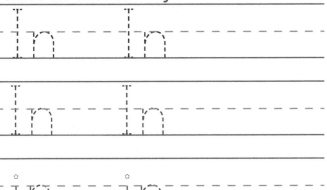

Color the spaces with the word:

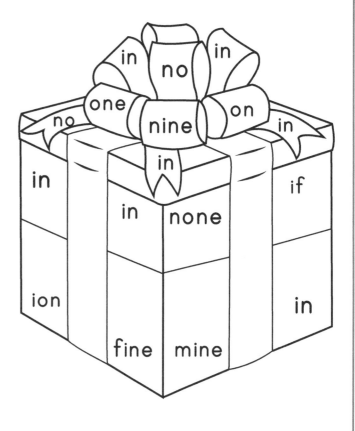

Write the word on your own:

Cut out the word at the bottom of the page and paste it here to complete the sentence:

My gift is ⸬⸬ a box.

Complete the sentence with the word:

My gift is ___ a box.

Write your own sentence using the word:

i n

Trace the word and say it aloud:

Is Is

Is Is

is is

is is

Write the word on your own:

Color the spaces with the word:

is
miss
in
is
sit   12   in
11   1
10   is   2
in 9   sis   3   if
his
8   is   4
7   5   it
6
is
ice

Cut out the word at the bottom of the page and paste it here to complete the sentence:

What time [   ] it?

Complete the sentence with the word:

What time ___ it?

Write your own sentence using the word:

i s

it

Trace the word and say it aloud:

Color the spaces with the word:

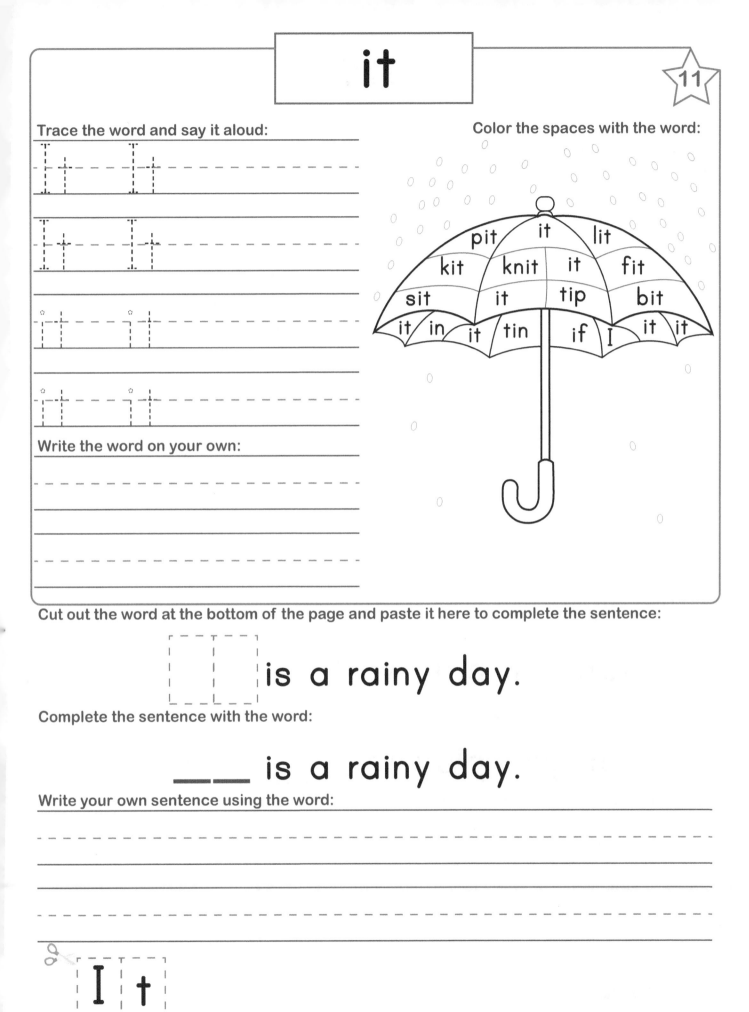

pit   it   lit
kit   knit   it   fit
sit   it   tip   bit
it   in   it   tin   if   I   it   it

Write the word on your own:

Cut out the word at the bottom of the page and paste it here to complete the sentence:

☐ is a rainy day.

Complete the sentence with the word:

_____ is a rainy day.

Write your own sentence using the word:

✂ I t

me

Trace the word and say it aloud:

Me Me

Me Me

me me

me me

Write the word on your own:

Color the spaces with the word:

med

my

my aim

me

ma

men be

me

mine

me

a see

met

me

my

mug

Cut out the word at the bottom of the page and paste it here to complete the sentence:

Can you play with ⬚ ?

Complete the sentence with the word:

Can you play with ___ ?

Write your own sentence using the word:

m e

my

Trace the word and say it aloud:

My My
My My
my my
my my

Write the word on your own:

Color the spaces with the word:

by
my
yam
my
a
may
my
yum
me
my
a
by
my
my
ma

Cut out the word at the bottom of the page and paste it here to complete the sentence:

I love ⬚ fish.

Complete the sentence with the word:

I love ___ fish.

Write your own sentence using the word:

m y

no

Trace the word and say it aloud:

No No No

No No No

no no no

no no no

Write the word on your own:

Color the spaces with the word:

Cut out the word at the bottom of the page and paste it here to complete the sentence:

" ⬚⬚ ," said the elf.

Complete the sentence with the word:

" ___ ," said the elf.

Write your own sentence using the word:

N o

on

Trace the word and say it aloud:

On On On

On On On

on on on

on on on

Write the word on your own:

Color the spaces with the word:

Cut out the word at the bottom of the page and paste it here to complete the sentence:

Books are [ ] the shelf.

Complete the sentence with the word:

Books are ____ the shelf.

Write your own sentence using the word:

o n

SO

Trace the word and say it aloud:

So So So
So So So
So So so
so so so

Write the word on your own:

Color the spaces with the word:

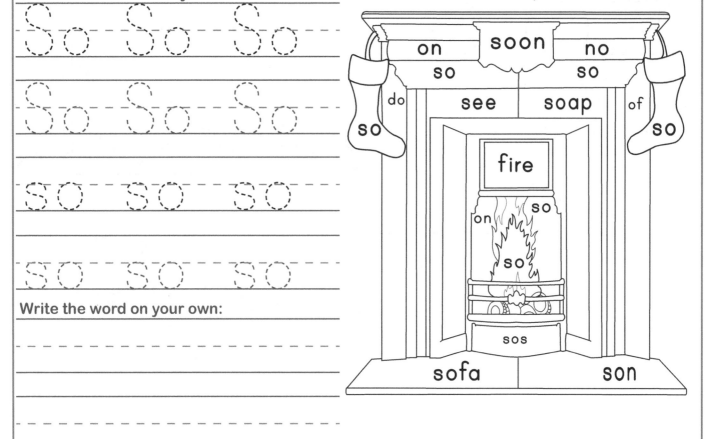

on soon no
so so
do see soap of
so so

fire
on so
so

sos

sofa son

Cut out the word at the bottom of the page and paste it here to complete the sentence:

It's [ ] warm in here.

Complete the sentence with the word:

It's ___ warm in here.

Write your own sentence using the word:

s o

to

Trace the word and say it aloud:

To To To

To To To

to to to

to to to

Write the word on your own:

Color the spaces with the word:

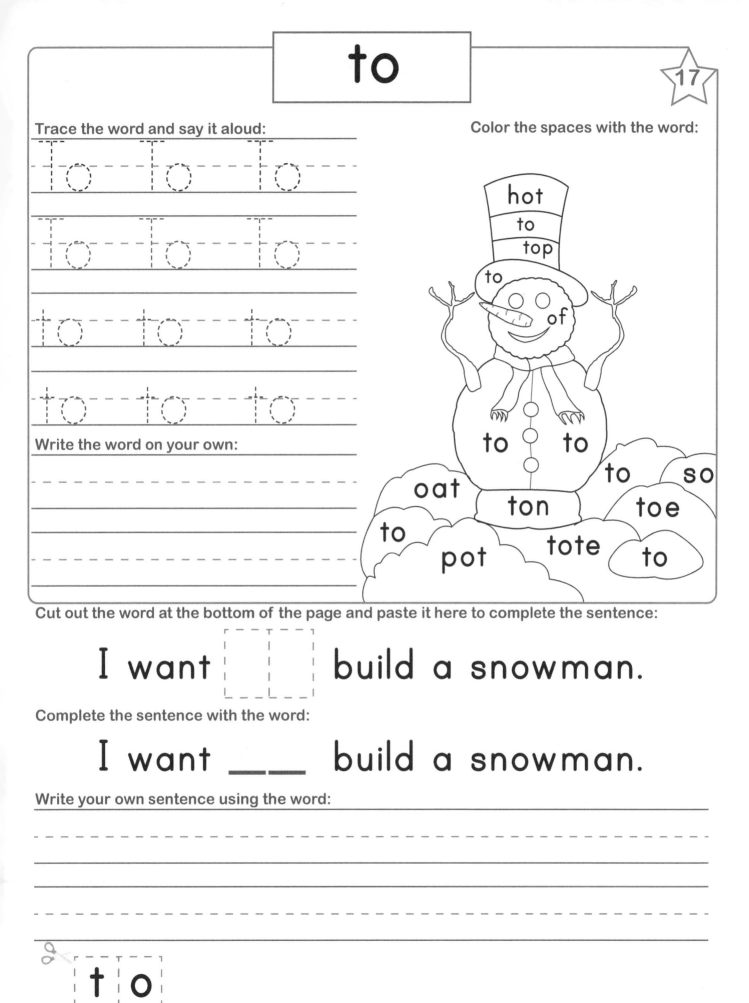

Cut out the word at the bottom of the page and paste it here to complete the sentence:

I want ☐☐ build a snowman.

Complete the sentence with the word:

I want ___ build a snowman.

Write your own sentence using the word:

✂ t o

up

Trace the word and say it aloud:

Up Up Up

Up Up Up

up up up

up up up

Write the word on your own:

Color the spaces with the word:

up

us

up up

us us

up

up

pup

up cup

put

up

us

up open pun

cup up

Cut out the word at the bottom of the page and paste it here to complete the sentence:

The kite can go ☐☐ and away.

Complete the sentence with the word:

The kite can go ___ and away.

Write your own sentence using the word:

u p

we

Trace the word and say it aloud:

We We
We We
we we
we we

Write the word on your own:

Color the spaces with the word:

we	awe	we
vet	well	whee
went	we	wet
we	row	
were	awe	be

we · we · we · row · be · we

Cut out the word at the bottom of the page and paste it here to complete the sentence:

Can ☐ visit a farm?

Complete the sentence with the word:

Can ___ visit a farm?

Write your own sentence using the word:

we

all

Trace the word and say it aloud:

All All

All All

all all

all all

Write the word on your own:

Color the spaces with the word:

at
all
all
a
fall
an
at
are all an a
a
all
mall
all
an

Cut out the word at the bottom of the page and paste it here to complete the sentence:

the birds flew away.

Complete the sentence with the word:

_____ the birds flew away.

Write your own sentence using the word:

All

and

 21

Trace the word and say it aloud:

And And

And And

and and

and and

Write the word on your own:

Color the spaces with the word:

are

an

and

an

and

and

band

can

den

and

nod

bard

an

are

and   and

and

Cut out the word at the bottom of the page and paste it here to complete the sentence:

I see a whale [ ] a quail.

Complete the sentence with the word:

I see a whale _____ a quail.

Write your own sentence using the word:

and

any

Trace the word and say it aloud:

Any Any

Any Any

any any

any any

Write the word on your own:

Color the spaces with the word:

any   amy   any

any   many

all   are   and

and   an

nay   any

Cut out the word at the bottom of the page and paste it here to complete the sentence:

Do you have ⬚⬚⬚ cookies?

Complete the sentence with the word:

Do you have ____ cookies?

Write your own sentence using the word:

a n y

are

Trace the word and say it aloud:

Are Are

Are Are

are are

are are

Write the word on your own:

Color the spaces with the word:

an
are
am
are
an
a
are
at
are
ate
are
am

Cut out the word at the bottom of the page and paste it here to complete the sentence:

These ☐☐☐ my toys.

Complete the sentence with the word:

These _____ my toys.

Write your own sentence using the word:

a r e

big

Trace the word and say it aloud:

Big Big

Big Big

big big

big big

Write the word on your own:

Color the spaces with the word:

Cut out the word at the bottom of the page and paste it here to complete the sentence:

Elephants are ☐☐☐ .

Complete the sentence with the word:

Elephants are _____ .

Write your own sentence using the word:

b i g

can

Trace the word and say it aloud:

Can Can

Can Can

can can

can can

Write the word on your own:

Color the spaces with the word:

can
can

can
cane   an
        and
a   can
    can
        an

can
man
        can
        can

Cut out the word at the bottom of the page and paste it here to complete the sentence:

Cheetahs [   ] run fast.

Complete the sentence with the word:

Cheetahs _____ run fast.

Write your own sentence using the word:

c a n

day

Trace the word and say it aloud:

Day Day

Day Day

day day

day day

Write the word on your own:

Color the spaces with the word:

day | bay
say | day
dad | day | aye
day | day
pay | yet
day | day
day
ad as
bay | day | a | can | day

Cut out the word at the bottom of the page and paste it here to complete the sentence:

Today is Valentine's [   ] .

Complete the sentence with the word:

Today is Valentine's _____ .

Write your own sentence using the word:

did

Trace the word and say it aloud:

Did Did

Did Did

did did

did did

Write the word on your own:

Color the spaces with the word:

dad
bib
bid
dib
hide
did
did
din
did
aid
rid
did
day
bib
did
day
dad

Cut out the word at the bottom of the page and paste it here to complete the sentence:

☐ you feed the duck?

Complete the sentence with the word:

_____ you feed the duck?

Write your own sentence using the word:

Trace the word and say it aloud:

Eat Eat

Eat Eat

eat eat

eat eat

Write the word on your own:

Color the spaces with the word:

heat
tea
eat
feat
eel
eat
a
teal
meal
rat
at
eat
eat

eat

treat

meat

Cut out the word at the bottom of the page and paste it here to complete the sentence:

Dolphins ☐☐☐ fish.

Complete the sentence with the word:

Dolphins _____ fish.

Write your own sentence using the word:

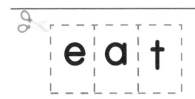

Trace the word and say it aloud:

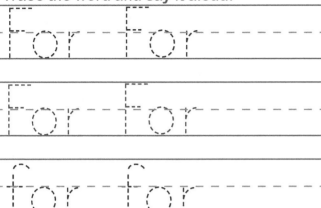

For For
For For
for for
for for

Write the word on your own:

Color the spaces with the word:

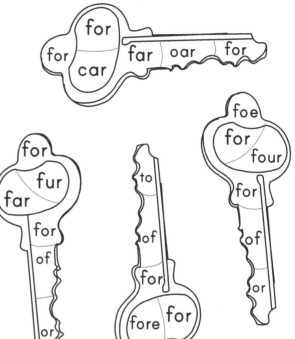

Cut out the word at the bottom of the page and paste it here to complete the sentence:

Can you search ☐☐☐ my keys?

Complete the sentence with the word:

Can you search _____ my keys?

Write your own sentence using the word:

f o r

get

Trace the word and say it aloud:

Get Get

Get Get

get get

get get

Write the word on your own:

Color the spaces with the word:

get	set	ten	debt
gait	tag	got	get
got	jet	get	tong
get	gal	get	ten
gen	goat	gel	debt
hot	lot	got	met
go	etc	get	pet

Cut out the word at the bottom of the page and paste it here to complete the sentence:

Can I ☐☐☐ the crayons?

Complete the sentence with the word:

Can I _ _ _ _ the crayons?

Write your own sentence using the word:

has

Trace the word and say it aloud:

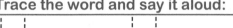

Has Has

Has Has

has has

has has

Write the word on your own:

Color the spaces with the word:

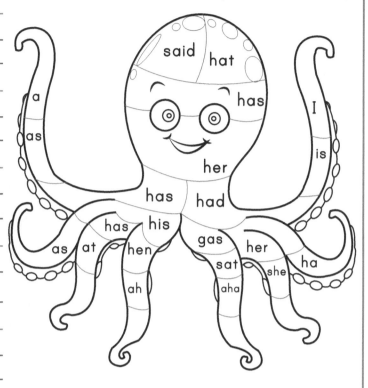

Cut out the word at the bottom of the page and paste it here to complete the sentence:

An octopus [ ] eight limbs.

Complete the sentence with the word:

An octopus _____ eight limbs.

Write your own sentence using the word:

✂ h a s

Trace the word and say it aloud:

How How

How How

how how

how how

Write the word on your own:

Color the spaces with the word:

how   our
hue
how
whoo
who

ha he

hue   hoot

have   why

sow   wow
how   pow
aha   how

Cut out the word at the bottom of the page and paste it here to complete the sentence:

many mice do you see?

Complete the sentence with the word:

_____ many mice do you see?

Write your own sentence using the word:

How

may

Trace the word and say it aloud:

May May

May May

may may

may may

Write the word on your own:

Color the spaces with the word:

| am | may | aim | man |

| may | name | may | nay |

| me | aye | mane | may |

| may | may | may | mam |

| me | may | may | yam |

Cut out the word at the bottom of the page and paste it here to complete the sentence:

[   ] I use your pencils?

Complete the sentence with the word:

_____ I use your pencils?

Write your own sentence using the word:

May

new

Trace the word and say it aloud:

New New

New New

new new

new new

Write the word on your own:

Color the spaces with the word:

Boo!

new
no   win   nine   new
nest   net   new
few   nah
nil   new   we
new   dew   few   new

Cut out the word at the bottom of the page and paste it here to complete the sentence:

I have a [ ] costume.

Complete the sentence with the word:

I have a _____ costume.

Write your own sentence using the word:

now

Trace the word and say it aloud:

Now Now

Now Now

now now

now now

Write the word on your own:

Color the spaces with the word:

not now non
now
win wow won now
nose
now
now nor
one new
nah
no now

Cut out the word at the bottom of the page and paste it here to complete the sentence:

It is sunny right ☐☐☐ .

Complete the sentence with the word:

It is sunny right _____ .

Write your own sentence using the word:

n o w

our

Trace the word and say it aloud:

Our Our

Our Our

our our

our our

Write the word on your own:

Color the spaces with the word:

our
our
out
our
our
us
or
our
you
ear
our
pour
our
sour
you
four
our
hour
or
our
our
our

Cut out the word at the bottom of the page and paste it here to complete the sentence:

This is ☐☐☐ dog.

Complete the sentence with the word:

This is _____ dog.

Write your own sentence using the word:

o u r

Trace the word and say it aloud:

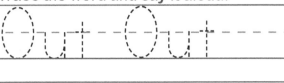

Color the spaces with the word:

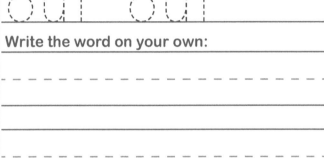

Write the word on your own:

Cut out the word at the bottom of the page and paste it here to complete the sentence:

Owls come [ ] at night.

Complete the sentence with the word:

Owls come ____ at night.

Write your own sentence using the word:

✂ o u t

ran

Trace the word and say it aloud:

Ran Ran

Ran Ran

ran ran

ran ran

Write the word on your own:

Color the spaces with the word:

ran
run ran
rat
rap
ran
run man arm can fan
urn rain ran
an
ran rant
ran
run

Cut out the word at the bottom of the page and paste it here to complete the sentence:

The deer [ ] away.

Complete the sentence with the word:

The deer _____ away.

Write your own sentence using the word:

r a n

saw

Trace the word and say it aloud:

Saw Saw

Saw Saw

saw saw

saw saw

Write the word on your own:

Color the spaces with the word:

as	saw
saw	awe	at
see	saw
saw	saw	is

saw

saw

saw is a am as

we is sigh was

said saw

saw saw whiz

saw sauve

Cut out the word at the bottom of the page and paste it here to complete the sentence:

I ☐☐☐ a lion at the zoo.

Complete the sentence with the word:

I _____ a lion at the zoo.

Write your own sentence using the word:

✂ s a w

say

Trace the word and say it aloud:

Say Say

Say Say

say say

say say

Write the word on your own:

Color the spaces with the word:

saw
yes
say
sun is
yay
said
sad stay
say spray
say sail
say
say say
say
is
so
say as sorry

Cut out the word at the bottom of the page and paste it here to complete the sentence:

I want to [ ] I'm sorry.

Complete the sentence with the word:

I want to _____ I'm sorry.

Write your own sentence using the word:

say

see

Trace the word and say it aloud:

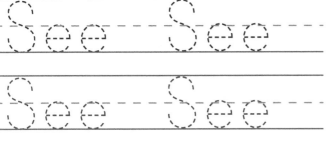

Write the word on your own:

Color the spaces with the word:

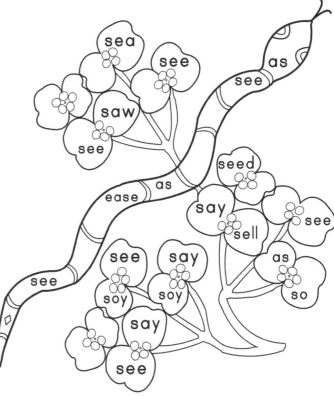

Cut out the word at the bottom of the page and paste it here to complete the sentence:

Can you [ ] the snake?

Complete the sentence with the word:

Can you _____ the snake?

Write your own sentence using the word:

s e e

the

Trace the word and say it aloud:

The The

The The

the the

the the

Write the word on your own:

Color the spaces with the word:

the | then | there | the
the | their | this | the
toe | ten | hat | hen
the | the
the | the
the | the
the
bathe
thin | the
the | that

Cut out the word at the bottom of the page and paste it here to complete the sentence:

[   ] cake is ready to eat.

Complete the sentence with the word:

_____ cake is ready to eat.

Write your own sentence using the word:

was

Trace the word and say it aloud:

Was Was

Was Was

was was

was was

Write the word on your own:

Color the spaces with the word:

was

whiz   as

has   vase
        was

saw | was
vow | wow

wall | what | war
was | few | was

Cut out the word at the bottom of the page and paste it here to complete the sentence:

The frog [   ] ready to jump.

Complete the sentence with the word:

The frog _____ ready to jump.

Write your own sentence using the word:

was

who

Trace the word and say it aloud:

Who Who

Who Who

who who

who who

Write the word on your own:

Color the spaces with the word:

he | how | we
who | how | who
who | what
who | who
how | have | however
who | why | whose
he | who | woohoo
Santa

Cut out the word at the bottom of the page and paste it here to complete the sentence:

am I?

Complete the sentence with the word:

_____ am I?

Write your own sentence using the word:

why

Trace the word and say it aloud:

Why Why

Why Why

why why

why why

Write the word on your own:

Color the spaces with the word:

who
what
why
how   wow   why
hay   whee
why
wohoo   have
whey   why
what   why
why   yay

Cut out the word at the bottom of the page and paste it here to complete the sentence:

can't penguins fly?

Complete the sentence with the word:

_____ can't penguins fly?

Write your own sentence using the word:

W h y

yes

Trace the word and say it aloud:

Yes Yes

Yes Yes

yes yes

yes yes

Write the word on your own:

Color the spaces with the word:

no
yes
yes   yes
yet yell
yes say
easy maybe
yes
so   soy yet
yak
yes
yes
yes
no no

Cut out the word at the bottom of the page and paste it here to complete the sentence:

[   ] , monkeys like bananas.

Complete the sentence with the word:

_____ , monkeys like bananas.

Write your own sentence using the word:

Yes

you

Trace the word and say it aloud:

You You
You You
you you
you you

Write the word on your own:

Color the spaces with the word:

yes
yoyo you
so yeah
you your
yum unicorn
soul on you young us
you yet oust
you use
you you
you
you

Cut out the word at the bottom of the page and paste it here to complete the sentence:

I love ⬚⬚⬚ .

Complete the sentence with the word:

I love _____ .

Write your own sentence using the word:

y o u

Part 2:
Learn to read & write
(4, 5, 6 Letter Sight Words)

- Say the word out loud
- Trace it and write it on your own
- Color the correct sight words.
- Cut out the letter cards along the dotted lines at the bottom of the page and **rearrange them to form the word**. Paste them in the right boxes to complete the sentence.
- Write the word to fill in the blanks.
- Use the word in a sentence

*Remember: A sentence begins with a capital letter and ends with a period.

You are AMAZING!

Celebrate your success!
Color a star at the end of the book to mark each word you have learnt.

away

Trace the word and say it aloud:

Away Away

Away Away

away away

away away

Write the word on your own:

Color the spaces with the word:

away

we

away

away

an

way

away

yay

way

awe

yae

away

Cut out the letters at the bottom of the page and rearrange them to form the word.
Paste it here to complete the sentence:

Put your hat ☐☐☐☐ .

Complete the sentence with the word:

Put your hat _____ .

Write your own sentence using the word:

w a a y

blue

Trace the word and say it aloud:

Blue   Blue

Blue   Blue

blue   blue

blue   blue

Write the word on your own:

Color the spaces with the word:

drew

dew blew

blue

blue

due

bell blue

clue

blue

be

blue

duel

blue

blue

brew

Cut out the letters at the bottom of the page and rearrange them to form the word.
Paste it here to complete the sentence:

I love the ⬚⬚⬚⬚ sky.

Complete the sentence with the word:

I love the _____ sky.

Write your own sentence using the word:

u l e b

come

Trace the word and say it aloud:

Come Come

Come Come

come come

come come

Write the word on your own:

Color the spaces with the word:

coup
ma
a
mock
came
calm
code
foam
come
am
cane
me
me
some
cone
come
come
comet
come
core
came
cool

Cut out the letters at the bottom of the page and rearrange them to form the word.
Paste it here to complete the sentence:

Please ☐☐☐☐ see this snail.

Complete the sentence with the word:

Please _____ see this snail.

Write your own sentence using the word:

down

Trace the word and say it aloud:

Down Down

Down Down

down down

down down

Write the word on your own:

Color the spaces with the word:

dawn | down
up | came | up
down | own
own
clown
owe | dough | won | do
on
don | down | own
down | dawn | down
won | down | wind

Cut out the letters at the bottom of the page and rearrange them to form the word.
Paste it here to complete the sentence:

This panda is sitting ⬚⬚⬚⬚ .

Complete the sentence with the word:

This panda is sitting _____ .

Write your own sentence using the word:

w o n d

find

Trace the word and say it aloud:

find   find

find   find

find   find

find   find

Write the word on your own:

Color the spaces with the word:

fin
find
fine

define

find

wind

find

dine

den

in
fan
nod

find
fond
din

rind

fad

find

find

bind

fine
fend
find

mind

Cut out the letters at the bottom of the page and rearrange them to form the word.
Paste it here to complete the sentence:

Can you ⌞ ⌞ ⌞ ⌞ ⌟ the eggs?

Complete the sentence with the word:

Can you _____ the eggs?

Write your own sentence using the word:

f d n i

give

 53

Trace the word and say it aloud:

Give   Give

Give   Give

give   give

give   give

Write the word on your own:

Color the spaces with the word:

give
gave
vie
veg
go
wage   gee

we
give   live
give   five   go

I   give
jive

Cut out the letters at the bottom of the page and rearrange them to form the word.
Paste it here to complete the sentence:

Please [ ] me a candy.

Complete the sentence with the word:

Please _____ me a candy.

Write your own sentence using the word:

i g v e

Trace the word and say it aloud:

Good Good

Good Good

good good

good good

Write the word on your own:

Color the spaces with the word:

give
goo
good
goof
ago   dig
dog
glad
good   dog
give
mood
give
do
good   glow   food
gal   glue   give
go give gone bad
do god give gee
go ode goon go

Cut out the letters at the bottom of the page and rearrange them to form the word.
Paste it here to complete the sentence:

Ice-cream tastes ⸤   ⸥ .

Complete the sentence with the word:

Ice-cream tastes _____ .

Write your own sentence using the word:

o g o d

grow

Trace the word and say it aloud:

Grow Grow

Grow Grow

grow grow

grow grow

Write the word on your own:

Color the spaces with the word:

gray
grow
grey
grow
grew
grown
grow
grin
grow
grow show
brow
grow
grow
go
grow
row wag
ago
woe
or
ore

Cut out the letters at the bottom of the page and rearrange them to form the word.
Paste it here to complete the sentence:

Sunflowers ☐☐☐☐ big and tall.

Complete the sentence with the word:

Sunflowers _____ big and tall.

Write your own sentence using the word:

have

Trace the word and say it aloud:

Have Have

Have Have

have have

have have

Write the word on your own:

Color the spaces with the word:

hive

gave

have

weave

hat

how

has

have

had

shave

have

have

ah

have

who

have

aha

who

have

how

hover

ahead

heavy

heave

Cut out the letters at the bottom of the page and rearrange them to form the word.
Paste it here to complete the sentence:

I ⬚⬚⬚⬚ a pet pig.

Complete the sentence with the word:

I _____ a pet pig.

Write your own sentence using the word:

h a e v

help

Trace the word and say it aloud:

Help   Help

Help   Help

help   help

help   help

Write the word on your own:

Color the spaces with the word:

help
he   kelp
pelt
help
helper
hip
helps
helped
hall
help
elf   elves hen
help
held   hold
herald   help he
hep
play
help

Cut out the letters at the bottom of the page and rearrange them to form the word.
Paste it here to complete the sentence:

I need ⬚⬚⬚⬚ to decorate the tree.

Complete the sentence with the word:

I need _____ to decorate the tree.

Write your own sentence using the word:

p e h l

here

Trace the word and say it aloud:

Here   Here

Here   Here

here   here

here   hee

Write the word on your own:

Color the spaces with the word:

here

her
here
hear
he
hi
hare
eve
hairy   hair
heard
there   where
the   here   here
reed
were
eerie

Cut out the letters at the bottom of the page and rearrange them to form the word.
Paste it here to complete the sentence:

The Easter Bunny is ⬚⬚⬚⬚ .

Complete the sentence with the word:

The Easter Bunny is _____ .

Write your own sentence using the word:

e r e h

hold

Trace the word and say it aloud:

Hold Hold

Hold Hold

hold hold

hold hold

Write the word on your own:

Color the spaces with the word:

old
do
hold
behold
hold hold lo
told cold fold mold sold hold
hold doll lord
ode hole
hold held

Cut out the letters at the bottom of the page and rearrange them to form the word.
Paste it here to complete the sentence:

This basket can ⬚⬚⬚⬚ fruits.

Complete the sentence with the word:

This basket can _____ fruits.

Write your own sentence using the word:

into

Trace the word and say it aloud:

Into   Into

Into   Into

into   into

into   into

Write the word on your own:

Color the spaces with the word:

nit | tint
knit
into | into
tin | into

hint | coin
mint
into | knot
lint | into

into | ton   not | into
into | in   tin | into
ant   into
pronto   ion
into   tint

Cut out the letters at the bottom of the page and rearrange them to form the word.
Paste it here to complete the sentence:

A caterpillar turns [ ] a butterfly.

Complete the sentence with the word:

A caterpillar turns _____ a butterfly.

Write your own sentence using the word:

o   i   t   n

jump

Trace the word and say it aloud:

Jump Jump

Jump Jump

jump jump

jump jump

Write the word on your own:

Color the spaces with the word:

jump
up
jump
jumped
juice   jump
jumps   puma
jump
jumping
jump   jumper
jeep
pump

jump / pup
up / jam

jump / jinx

jump

Cut out the letters at the bottom of the page and rearrange them to form the word.
Paste it here to complete the sentence:

Kangaroos can ⬚⬚⬚⬚ very high.

Complete the sentence with the word:

Kangaroos can _____ very high.

Write your own sentence using the word:

✂ u m j p

keep

Trace the word and say it aloud:

Keep keep

Keep keep

keep keep

keep keep

Write the word on your own:

Color the spaces with the word:

kip

key

keep

keeper   keeps

keep   kept

keep

keep

keeping

pep

keep

keep   keep   keep   peck

keep   eke

peeked

seep

Cut out the letters at the bottom of the page and rearrange them to form the word.
Paste it here to complete the sentence:

Can I ⬚⬚⬚⬚ this iguana?

Complete the sentence with the word:

Can I _____ this iguana?

Write your own sentence using the word:

Trace the word and say it aloud:

Kind   Kind

Kind   Kind

kind   kind

kind   kind

Write the word on your own:

Color the spaces with the word:

din   kind   kind
        do
kinder
kiln   kind
kind   rind
send   mind
kin
find   kind   in
kind   kilt
kids   kind
kindest   kinder

Cut out the letters at the bottom of the page and rearrange them to form the word.
Paste it here to complete the sentence:

My carpet is one of a ⬚⬚⬚⬚ .

Complete the sentence with the word:

My carpet is one of a _____ .

Write your own sentence using the word:

like

Trace the word and say it aloud:

Like   Like

Like   Like

like   like

like   like

Write the word on your own:

Color the spaces with the word:

liken

like   spike

tyke like like   licks

licked lick li'l   liked

likes kite lie   like

like   like   like

ill lie ail

like

eke like

bike kite like

lies lice likes link

Cut out the letters at the bottom of the page and rearrange them to form the word.
Paste it here to complete the sentence: _____

I ⌐ ¬ to go trick or treating.

Complete the sentence with the word:

I _____ to go trick or treating.

Write your own sentence using the word:

Trace the word and say it aloud:

Live   Live

Live   Live

live   live

live   live

Write the word on your own:

Color the spaces with the word:

live
liven
lives
live   live   live
line
vie
will   I
life   live   vile
live
live

liver   line   lived   live
lite   lived   well   live   live
live   Nile   veil   yell
veiled   live   lives

Cut out the letters at the bottom of the page and rearrange them to form the word.
Paste it here to complete the sentence:

Turtles ☐☐☐☐ in the sea.

Complete the sentence with the word:

Turtles _____ in the sea.

Write your own sentence using the word:

✂ l v e i

look

Trace the word and say it aloud:

Look Look

Look Look

look look

look look

Write the word on your own:

Color the spaces with the word:

look   look

look   lock   look

no   look   spool   lock

look   looking spook   look

old

looked   nook   wok   lo

look   nook

Cut out the letters at the bottom of the page and rearrange them to form the word.
Paste it here to complete the sentence:

[ ][ ][ ][ ] at this pot of gold.

Complete the sentence with the word:

_ _ _ _ at this pot of gold.

Write your own sentence using the word:

k o L o

make

Trace the word and say it aloud:

Make Make

Make Make

make make

make make

Write the word on your own:

Color the spaces with the word:

make
make
ma
made wake
makes make cakes
rake take make
came make come
make karma
make make mock
mode make meek
make

Cut out the letters at the bottom of the page and rearrange them to form the word.
Paste it here to complete the sentence:

Bees ☐☐☐☐ honey.

Complete the sentence with the word:

Bees _____ honey.

Write your own sentence using the word:

many

Trace the word and say it aloud:

Many Many

Many Many

many many

many many

Write the word on your own:

Color the spaces with the word:

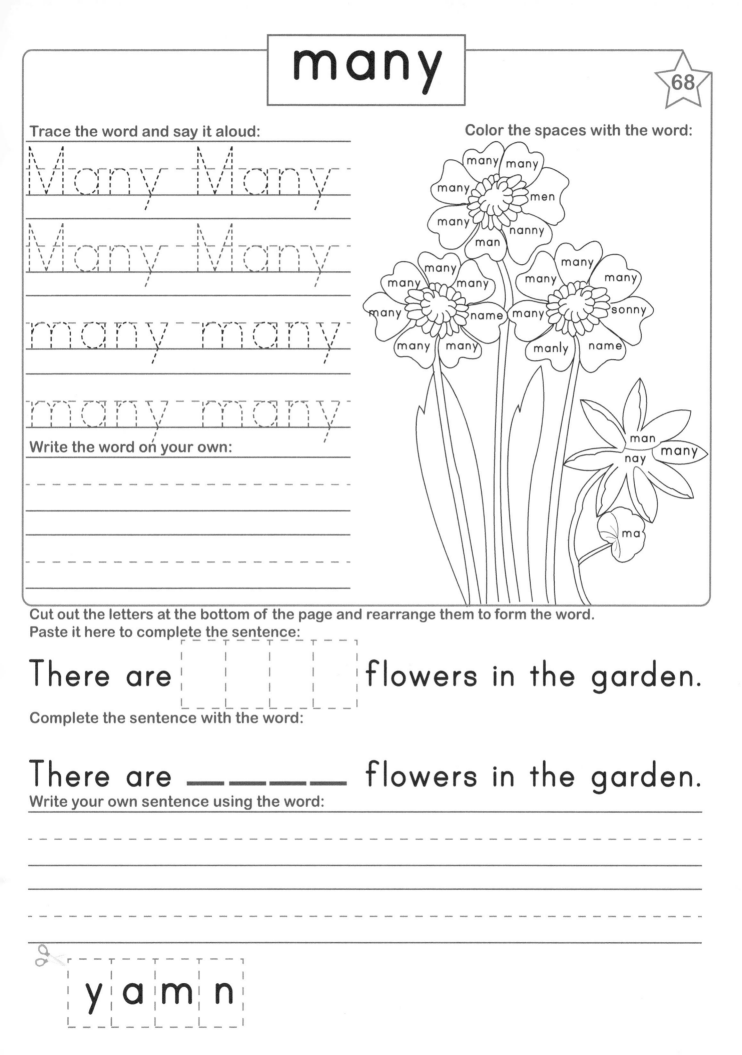

Cut out the letters at the bottom of the page and rearrange them to form the word.
Paste it here to complete the sentence:

There are [　　　] flowers in the garden.

Complete the sentence with the word:

There are _____ flowers in the garden.

Write your own sentence using the word:

y a m n

most

Trace the word and say it aloud:

Most Most

Most Most

most most

most most

Write the word on your own:

Color the spaces with the word:

must
me
so
sum
most
mist   most
rust   storm   moss
mast   must   most
to
most   most
most   met   so   must
atom   mast

Cut out the letters at the bottom of the page and rearrange them to form the word.
Paste it here to complete the sentence:

I like giraffes the ⬚⬚⬚⬚ .

Complete the sentence with the word:

I like giraffes the _____ .

Write your own sentence using the word:

m o t s

must

Trace the word and say it aloud:

Must Must

Must Must

must must

must must

Write the word on your own:

Color the spaces with the word:

most
must
must
moist
must
must
must
must
moisten
must
must
mush
tummy
krill
mast
mist
mostly
must
must
mash
mat
must
stem
mash

Cut out the letters at the bottom of the page and rearrange them to form the word.
Paste it here to complete the sentence:

The whale ☐☐☐☐ be hungry.

Complete the sentence with the word:

The whale _____ be hungry.

Write your own sentence using the word:

t u m s

Trace the word and say it aloud:

Over Over

Over Over

over over

over over

Write the word on your own:

Color the spaces with the word:

ever
over   or
over
over   clever
over
over   over
over
over   over
over
were
love
over

over | overtly | clover | veer
over | over | mover | over
beaver | mower | over | ever

Cut out the letters at the bottom of the page and rearrange them to form the word.
Paste it here to complete the sentence:

The bear went ⬚⬚⬚⬚ the mountain.

Complete the sentence with the word:

The bear went _____ the mountain.

Write your own sentence using the word:

✂ o r e v

read

Trace the word and say it aloud:

Read Read

Read Read

read read

read read

Write the word on your own:

Color the spaces with the word:

red	read

read	read	ready
reed		
dear	bread	creed
bear	raid	read
dread		
read		
dare		
read		
dear		
ride		

Cut out the letters at the bottom of the page and rearrange them to form the word.
Paste it here to complete the sentence:

I like to ☐☐☐☐ about animals.

Complete the sentence with the word:

I like to _____ about animals.

Write your own sentence using the word:

Trace the word and say it aloud:

Take   Take

Take   Take

take   take

take   take

Write the word on your own:

Color the spaces with the word:

green
orange
yellow
green
blue
indigo
violet

rake
take

take
cake

tea	key
tyke	truck
kite	takes	taken	take
take	take	taker	teak
took	take	intake	take

Cut out the letters at the bottom of the page and rearrange them to form the word.
Paste it here to complete the sentence:

a look at the rainbow.

Complete the sentence with the word:

_____ a look at the rainbow.

Write your own sentence using the word:

k a T e

that

Trace the word and say it aloud:

That That

That That

that that

that that

Write the word on your own:

Color the spaces with the word:

that
this
that
that
that that
that this thank hat
that that
that thought that tea
the ha
then the that
there that
the

Cut out the letters at the bottom of the page and rearrange them to form the word.
Paste it here to complete the sentence:

_____ is Rudolph the reindeer.

Complete the sentence with the word:

_____ is Rudolph the reindeer.

Write your own sentence using the word:

t T a h

this

Trace the word and say it aloud:

This   This

This   This

this   this

this   this

Write the word on your own:

Color the spaces with the word:

that
this
these
this
his
sit
this

hit
their | this | sheet | this
those | thirst | this | this | hits
the | he | this | than

Cut out the letters at the bottom of the page and rearrange them to form the word.
Paste it here to complete the sentence:

____ is a narwhal.

Complete the sentence with the word:

_____ is a narwhal.

Write your own sentence using the word:

T h s i

want

Trace the word and say it aloud:

Want Want

Want Want

want want

want want

Write the word on your own:

Color the spaces with the word:

went				
wont	want	want	note	ant
want	went	wants	newt	wand
wanted	went	vent	not	want
wane	wart	went	want	wasp

Cut out the letters at the bottom of the page and rearrange them to form the word.
Paste it here to complete the sentence:

I ☐☐☐☐ a gingerbread house.

Complete the sentence with the word:

I _____ a gingerbread house.

Write your own sentence using the word:

w n a t

Trace the word and say it aloud:

Well Well

Well Well

well well

well well

Write the word on your own:

Color the spaces with the word:

wall

well

we

will

well

well

wet

will

we

ill

yell

wellness

well

wall

we

all

well

well

Cut out the letters at the bottom of the page and rearrange them to form the word.
Paste it here to complete the sentence:

This koala is not feeling ⬚⬚⬚⬚.

Complete the sentence with the word:

This koala is not feeling _____ .

Write your own sentence using the word:

l w l e

went

Trace the word and say it aloud:

Went Went

Went Went

went went

went went

Write the word on your own:

Color the spaces with the word:

want	vent	went
wants	vents	want
wanted	went	went
well	net	went
new	newt	went
sent	went	bent
van	ten	win

Cut out the letters at the bottom of the page and rearrange them to form the word.
Paste it here to complete the sentence:

We ⬚⬚⬚⬚ to see the swans.

Complete the sentence with the word:

We _____ to see the swans.

Write your own sentence using the word:

✂ t e n w

were

Trace the word and say it aloud:

Were Were

Were Were

were were

were were

Write the word on your own:

Color the spaces with the word:

| ware |
| were |
| where |
| were |
| here |

wear		
war		veer
reed	were	hair
wheel	was	were
ware	hare	raw	here

Cut out the letters at the bottom of the page and rearrange them to form the word.
Paste it here to complete the sentence:

The crabs ⬚⬚⬚⬚ walking sideways.

Complete the sentence with the word:

The crabs _____ walking sideways.

Write your own sentence using the word:

✂ | w | e | e | r |

what

Trace the word and say it aloud:

What What

What What

what what

what what

Write the word on your own:

Color the spaces with the word:

white	thaw	what	wit	wart
watt	what	were	wan	whit
hot	when	what	how	what
hat	what	where	what	where
tow	what	what	what	what

Cut out the letters at the bottom of the page and rearrange them to form the word.
Paste it here to complete the sentence:

can you make with yarn?

Complete the sentence with the word:

_____ can you make with yarn?

Write your own sentence using the word:

t h a W

when

Trace the word and say it aloud:

When When

When When

when when

when when

Write the word on your own:

Color the spaces with the word:

when

when

who

when when

how

home

when	where	new	he
which	when	hen	when

wean

Cut out the letters at the bottom of the page and rearrange them to form the word.
Paste it here to complete the sentence:

will he go home?

Complete the sentence with the word:

_____ will he go home?

Write your own sentence using the word:

W n h e

will

Trace the word and say it aloud:

Will Will

Will Will

will will

will will

Write the word on your own:

Color the spaces with the word:

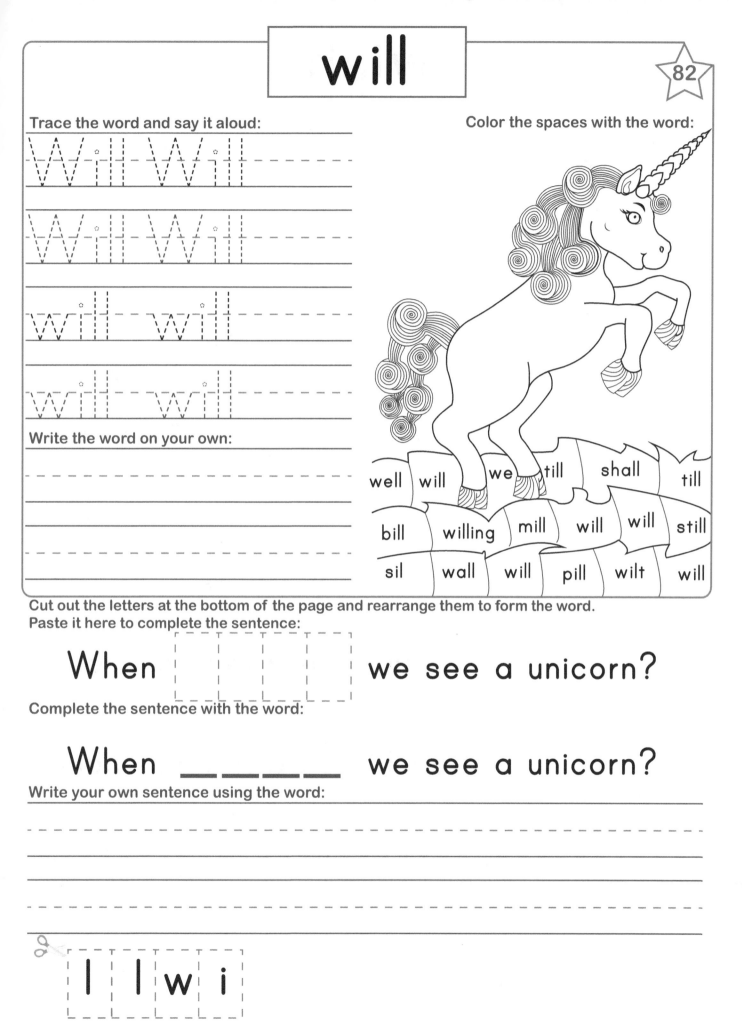

well	will	we	till	shall	till
bill	willing	mill	will	will	still
sil	wall	will	pill	wilt	will

Cut out the letters at the bottom of the page and rearrange them to form the word.
Paste it here to complete the sentence:

When ▯▯▯▯ we see a unicorn?

Complete the sentence with the word:

When _____ we see a unicorn?

Write your own sentence using the word:

✂ | l | l | w | i |

wish

Trace the word and say it aloud:

Wish Wish

Wish Wish

wish wish

wish wish

Write the word on your own:

Color the spaces with the word:

we	wash	swish	show
hi	wish	wish	mash

wish
shone wish wish
rash shin

hash	wish	show	wishing	wiz
sash	wish	sis	sew	wishes

Cut out the letters at the bottom of the page and rearrange them to form the word.
Paste it here to complete the sentence:

I ☐☐☐☐ I could see a real dinosaur.

Complete the sentence with the word:

I _____ I could see a real dinosaur.

Write your own sentence using the word:

i s w h

with

Trace the word and say it aloud:

With With

With With

with with

with with

Write the word on your own:

Color the spaces with the word:

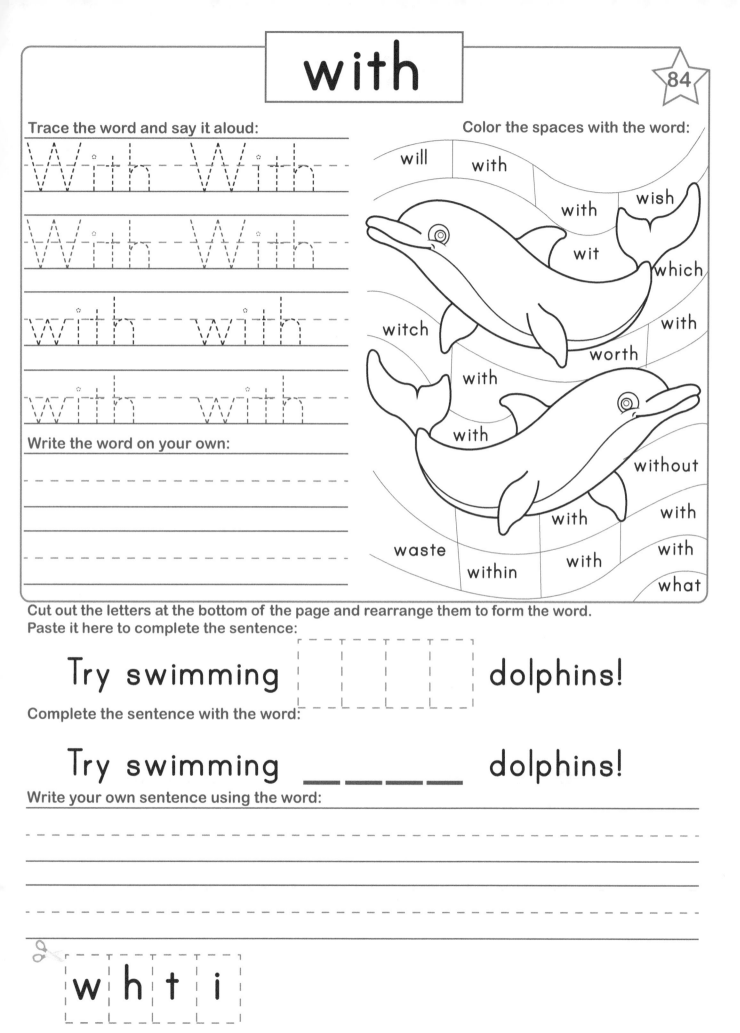

will · with · with · wish · wit · which · witch · with · worth · with · with · without · with · with · with · waste · within · with · what

Cut out the letters at the bottom of the page and rearrange them to form the word.
Paste it here to complete the sentence:

Try swimming [ ] [ ] [ ] [ ] dolphins!

Complete the sentence with the word:

Try swimming _____ dolphins!

Write your own sentence using the word:

w h t i

your

85

Trace the word and say it aloud:

Your Your

Your Your

your your

your your

Write the word on your own:

Color the spaces with the word:

your   your

my

yo

you

mine

me

few

your

your

yeah   yours

your your your   your

ours   ray   our

Cut out the letters at the bottom of the page and rearrange them to form the word.
Paste it here to complete the sentence:

Can you carve ⬚⬚⬚⬚ pumpkin?

Complete the sentence with the word:

Can you carve _____ pumpkin?

Write your own sentence using the word:

✂ y u r o

black

Trace the word and say it aloud:

Black Black

Black Black

black black

black black

Write the word on your own:

Color the spaces with the word:

black

bland

blue

rack

lack

black

bleak

black

black

white

black

black

blue

black

call

lab

black

slack

black

jack

black

black

Cut out the letters at the bottom of the page and rearrange them to form the word.
Paste it here to complete the sentence:

Those bats are _____ .

Complete the sentence with the word:

Those bats are _____ .

Write your own sentence using the word:

b c l a k

brown

Trace the word and say it aloud:

Brown Brown

Brown Brown

brown brown

brown brown

Write the word on your own:

Color the spaces with the word:

brown dawn
brown
brown
brown
row boar brow down
brow brown
bro
brown brew
brawn drawn
drawn drawn

Cut out the letters at the bottom of the page and rearrange them to form the word.
Paste it here to complete the sentence:

This is a [   ] bear.

Complete the sentence with the word:

This is a _____ bear.

Write your own sentence using the word:

o r w b n

every

Trace the word and say it aloud:

Every Every

Every Every

every every

every every

Write the word on your own:

Color the spaces with the word:

every	ever	very	every
rye	everyday		vary
		vary	
every		berry	every
	ward		
veer	eye	every	severe
every	each		every
		and	

Cut out the letters at the bottom of the page and rearrange them to form the word.
Paste it here to complete the sentence:

I did ☐☐☐☐☐ puzzle in class.

Complete the sentence with the word:

I did _____ puzzle in class.

Write your own sentence using the word:

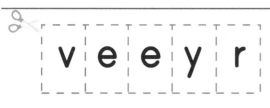

v e e y r

going

Trace the word and say it aloud:

Going Going

Going Going

going going

going going

Write the word on your own:

Color the spaces with the word:

gone | going
gong | oink | gosling
going | king | wing | goal
going | going | nagging | going
going | going | going

nag | going | sing | no

going | nog
ion | go

Cut out the letters at the bottom of the page and rearrange them to form the word.
Paste it here to complete the sentence:

I am ☐ ☐ ☐ ☐ ☐ to eat ice-cream.

Complete the sentence with the word:

I am _____ to eat ice-cream.

Write your own sentence using the word:

n g o g i

their

Trace the word and say it aloud:

Their Their

Their Their

their their

their their

Write the word on your own:

Color the spaces with the word:

there

their   rare

hair   the

heir

their   their

rite   they

their

there   height

their

this   their

Cut out the letters at the bottom of the page and rearrange them to form the word.
Paste it here to complete the sentence:

The eggs hatched in [ ] nest.

Complete the sentence with the word:

The eggs hatched in _____ nest.

Write your own sentence using the word:

t e i r h

under

Trace the word and say it aloud:

Under Under

Under Under

under under

under under

Write the word on your own:

Color the spaces with the word:

under

under

under

under

and

under

hinder

mender

minder

flounder

under

under

blunder

bender

dune

under

over

sender

Cut out the letters at the bottom of the page and rearrange them to form the word.
Paste it here to complete the sentence:

One bug is ☐☐☐☐☐ the leaf.

Complete the sentence with the word:

One bug is _____ the leaf.

Write your own sentence using the word:

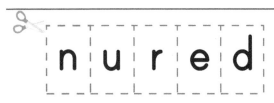
n u r e d

Trace the word and say it aloud:

Where

Where

where

where

Write the word on your own:

Color the spaces with the word:

how	where	hare	when	hear	what
her	here	ware	there	here	him
	wear	treasure	which	hare	
he	everywhere	when	here	eve	
	heard	where	aha	he	

Cut out the letters at the bottom of the page and rearrange them to form the word.
Paste it here to complete the sentence:

Maps show ☐☐☐☐☐ things are.

Complete the sentence with the word:

Maps show _____ things are.

Write your own sentence using the word:

✂ r h w e e

which

Trace the word and say it aloud:

Which

Which

which

which

Write the word on your own:

Color the spaces with the word:

hitch

where | which

whichever | when

which | chew | which

while | winch

how

watch | why

how | which

where

which

Cut out the letters at the bottom of the page and rearrange them to form the word.
Paste it here to complete the sentence:

color is your favorite?

Complete the sentence with the word:

_____ color is your favorite?

Write your own sentence using the word:

h c h W i

white

Trace the word and say it aloud:

White

White

white

white

Write the word on your own:

Color the spaces with the word:

while

whine

white
while

black

height

wait | white

tight | hide

sight | fight

which | wire

while | white

white | whit

white | hit

Cut out the letters at the bottom of the page and rearrange them to form the word.
Paste it here to complete the sentence:

Arctic foxes have ☐☐☐☐☐ coats.

Complete the sentence with the word:

Arctic foxes have _____ coats.

Write your own sentence using the word:

e t i w h

would

Trace the word and say it aloud:

Would

Would

would

would

Write the word on your own:

Color the spaces with the word:

mould	would		would
cold	should		
wood		ginger	bread
		would	could
		would	dow
would		would	weld
food		would	mood
told		will	would

Cut out the letters at the bottom of the page and rearrange them to form the word.
Paste it here to complete the sentence:

I [ ] [ ] [ ] [ ] [ ] like to bake this.

Complete the sentence with the word:

I _____ like to bake this.

Write your own sentence using the word:

d u l w o

Trace the word and say it aloud:

Number

Number

number

number

Write the word on your own:

Color the spaces with the word:

number	name	enabler
number	hunger	burn
numb	number	numbed
number	numbered	number
numbers	mumbler	lumber
numbering	slumber	number

Cut out the letters at the bottom of the page and rearrange them to form the word.
Paste it here to complete the sentence:

Count the ⸤　　　　　⸥ of ants.

Complete the sentence with the word:

Count the ＿＿＿＿＿ of ants.

Write your own sentence using the word:

u b e r m n

orange

Trace the word and say it aloud:

Orange

Orange

orange

orange

Write the word on your own:

Color the spaces with the word:

rang	ran	rain
nag	ore	ran
orange	orange	orange
or	ran	range
	ire	ran

rant	orange	nine	ring
oral	orangutan	orange	ting
ring	orange	orange	rant

Cut out the letters at the bottom of the page and rearrange them to form the word. Paste it here to complete the sentence:

Carrots are ⬚⬚⬚⬚⬚⬚ .

Complete the sentence with the word:

Carrots are _____ .

Write your own sentence using the word:

r e a n g o

please

Trace the word and say it aloud:

Please

Please

please

please

Write the word on your own:

Color the spaces with the word:

please

peas

please

lease	pea	sale	please	seal
pleasing	pleased	lace	ease	seep
place	please	see	please	sell

Cut out the letters at the bottom of the page and rearrange them to form the word.
Paste it here to complete the sentence:

☐☐☐☐☐☐ feed the fish.

Complete the sentence with the word:

_ _ _ _ _ _ feed the fish.

Write your own sentence using the word:

P e a s e l

pretty

Trace the word and say it aloud:

Pretty

Pretty

pretty

pretty

Write the word on your own:

Color the spaces with the word:

	pretty		
pretty	patty	try	pro
petty	trip	pretty	
pretty	gritty	pretty	pretty
witty	pretty	please	pity

Cut out the letters at the bottom of the page and rearrange them to form the word.
Paste it here to complete the sentence:

The rose is ⬜⬜⬜⬜⬜⬜ .

Complete the sentence with the word:

The rose is _____ .

Write your own sentence using the word:

t r e p t y

Trace the word and say it aloud:

Yellow

Yellow

yellow

yellow

Write the word on your own:

Color the spaces with the word:

yell

yellow

low

hello	yellow		wallow
fellow	yellow	yellow	halo
willow	will	mellow	yellow
ill	yellow	elbow	bellow

Cut out the letters at the bottom of the page and rearrange them to form the word.
Paste it here to complete the sentence:

corn is tasty.

Complete the sentence with the word:

_____ corn is tasty.

Write your own sentence using the word:

100 Sight Words
Completed ✓

Recommended next skills

ISBN: 1777421152

ISBN: 1679103709

Color a star after completing a page to track how much you have finished! Great Going!

1	2	3	4	5	6	7	8	9	10
11	12	13	14	15	16	17	18	19	20
21	22	23	24	25	26	27	28	29	30
31	32	33	34	35	36	37	38	39	40
41	42	43	44	45	46	47	48	49	50
51	52	53	54	55	56	57	58	59	60
61	62	63	64	65	66	67	68	69	70
71	72	73	74	75	76	77	78	79	80
81	82	83	84	85	86	87	88	89	90
91	92	93	94	95	96	97	98	99	100

Celebrate your Success!

Share the Joy!

Feel Great Everyday!

Write to me at **sujatha.lalgudi@gmail.com** with the subject:
100 Sight Words along with **your kid's name** to receive:

- Additional practice worksheets.
- A name tracing worksheet so your kid can practice writing their own name.
- An Award Certificate in Color to gift your child!

- ✂

Congratulations
Reading Super Star
Awarded to

_____

For _____

Date _____   Signed _____

Made in United States
Cleveland, OH
26 November 2024

10952505R00059